AN INTRODUCTION
JAZZ
CHORD VOICING
FOR KEYBOARD

BY BILL BOYD

ISBN-13: 978-1-4234-1773-6
ISBN-10: 1-4234-1773-9

HAL•LEONARD®
CORPORATION
7777 W. BLUEMOUND RD. P.O. BOX 13819 MILWAUKEE, WI 53213

In Australia Contact:
Hal Leonard Australia Pty. Ltd.
4 Lentara Court
Cheltenham, Victoria, 3192 Australia
Email: ausadmin@halleonard.com

Visit Hal Leonard Online at
www.halleonard.com

FOREWORD

The contemporary pianist is required to play solos and improvise accompaniments with chord voicings which are characteristic of today's jazz sound. This book teaches modern chord voicings and their application to solo and accompaniment playing.

Chord voicings are introduced in the context of the II V I chord progression in three major keys. A unique fingering system clarifies chord construction and aids the memory process. The appendices provide an excellent reference for chord voicings and chord progressions in all keys. The information in chapters thirteen and fourteen may be practically applied to actual jazz tunes.

There are two ways to approach the study of this book. Concentrate on chapters one through six and memorize the unaltered chords and progressions. Turn to Appendix A for a review of these chords in all keys and to Appendix B for the II V I progression in every key. Proceed to the remaining chapters and the appropriate appendices.

A second approach involves the completion of the entire book at once to develop facility in the three major keys which serve as examples in each chapter. Then refer to the appropriate appendices for supplementary study in other keys.

Mastery of the material in this book will improve performance and provide a background which will enable the pianist to better understand more advanced texts on the subject.

ABOUT THE CD

The accompanying CD features many of the examples in the book. In addition to representing the piano parts in the example, some tracks include a jazz ride pattern on the drumset or a full jazz rhythm section. These serve to help put each voicing example in a jazz context. Each track includes one measure of "clicks" before the example begins. An audio icon before the example indicates the corresponding track on the CD.

CONTENTS

1: CHORD CONSTRUCTION

A thorough knowledge of chord construction is not a prerequisite for the successful use of this book. All chords are labled and written out in every key. Chords should be memorized and facility moving from one to another developed through practice. A superficial knowledge of chord construction will aid the memorization process.

The major scale provides a basis for chord construction.

C MAJOR SCALE:

Chords are constructed by adding notes a third apart above the tones of a major scale:

Chords containing three notes are called TRIADS. The lowest note in the chord (the scale tone) is designated the ROOT. The remaining notes are identified by their relationship to the ROOT. Call the ROOT step "1" and count each space or line up to the second note in the chord. This note is on the third step above the root and is designated the THIRD. The next note is the FIFTH as it is on the fifth step above the root. Notes may be added which are on the seventh, ninth, eleventh and thirteenth steps above the root.

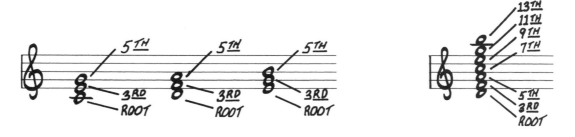

The chord names are determined by the letter name of the ROOT and by ROMAN NUMERALS which show the position of the chord in the scale.

Additional designations relate to the type of chord. There are four chord types or families:

MAJOR   MINOR   DOMINANT SEVENTH   DIMINISHED

A letter or Roman numeral alone designates a MAJOR triad. A small "m" indicates minor and "o" is diminished.

SEVENTH chords are constructed by adding a note seven scale steps above the root. Numbers are added to the designation to indicate additional notes in the chord.

(M7 = Major seventh   "7" = Dominant seventh   m7 = minor seventh)

NINTH chords are constructed by adding a note nine scale steps above the root.

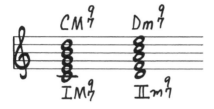

Throughout the book, chords will be labeled by letter or Roman numeral. These labels are called CHORD SYMBOLS.

CHORD SYMBOLS

MAJOR FAMILY	letter alone M7, Maj. 7, △	Major triad Major 7th chord
minor FAMILY	m7, min. 7, -7 m	minor 7th chord minor triad
DOMINANT 7th FAMILY	7 (pronounced "seventh")	Dominant 7th chord
DIMINISHED FAMILY	0 or dim.	Diminished triad or Diminished 7th chord

2: BASIC CHORD VOICINGS

The notes of the chord are regrouped for a better sound. This redistribution of the chord tones is called the CHORD VOICING. The possibilities for various chord voicings are endless. Therefore only two basic voicings are presented for each chord. These two voicings or POSITIONS were selected because:

they are the easiest to play and memorize.

all of the added and altered notes may be played.

they produce an idiomatic sound.

POSITION 1

The thumb of the right hand is ALWAYS on the 3rd of the chord. The second finger plays the 5th and the third finger plays the 7th. Memorize which finger plays each chord member as this is the fundamental fingering for all chords in Position 1. The left hand provides the chord root in both positions.

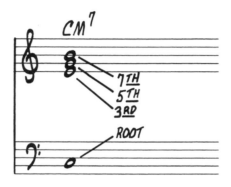

POSITION 2

The thumb of the right hand is ALWAYS on the 7th of the chord. The third finger is on the 3rd and the fifth finger is on the 5th. This fingering will remain the same for all types of chords in Position 2.

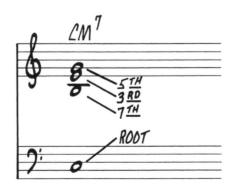
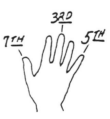

Think of Position 1 as the "position of the 3rd" and position 2 as the "position of the 7th."

The chord root may be played an octave lower.

The right hand may be played an octave lower if the sound is not "muddy."

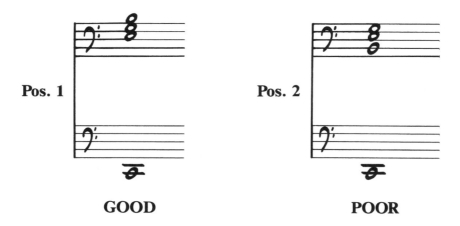

Chords may be played in various registers of the piano. Generally the sound is best when the right hand notes are within the area one octave above and below middle C.

When one chord moves to another the movement is called a CHORD PROGRESSION. Chord progressions are sometimes described in terms of the distance between one chord root and another. When chords move by half step, whole step or by thirds, select the same chord voicing or position for each chord.

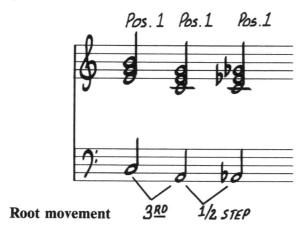

All of the right hand notes are fingered alike.

The movement from one chord to another should be as smooth as possible. Root movement by fourths and fifths would be awkward if the chords were played in the same position.

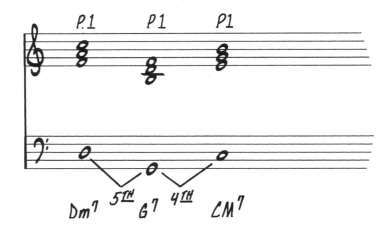

The movement from one chord to the other is smoother when Position 1 and Position 2 voicings are alternated.

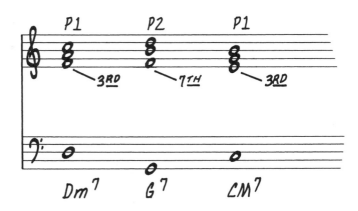

Many chord progressions contain root movement of a fourth or a fifth. The pianist must be well versed in both positions for each chord.

3: THE SEVENTH CHORDS

SEVENTH chords are constructed by adding to the triad the note which is seven scale steps above the root. Chords are easiest to memorize within the context of a progression. The II V I chord progression is one of the most common. The II chord is a minor seventh, the V is a dominant seventh and the I chord is a major seventh.

POSITION 1

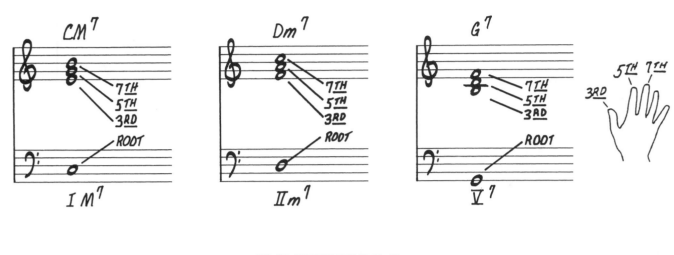

POSITION 2

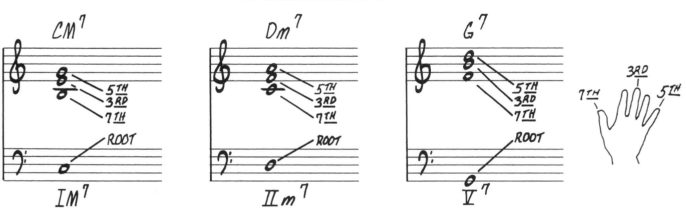

The following exercises are in the keys of "C", "F", and "Bb" major. Practice memorizing by playing the progressions over and over. Concentrate on the names of the chords and the notes contained in each. Use the correct fingerings and be aware of which finger plays the various chord members.

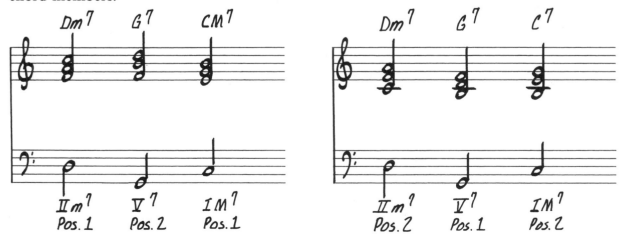

Chords in the key of F:

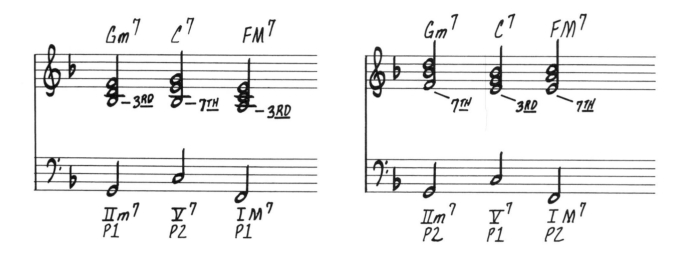

Chords in the key of B♭:

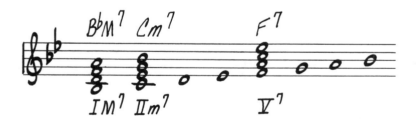

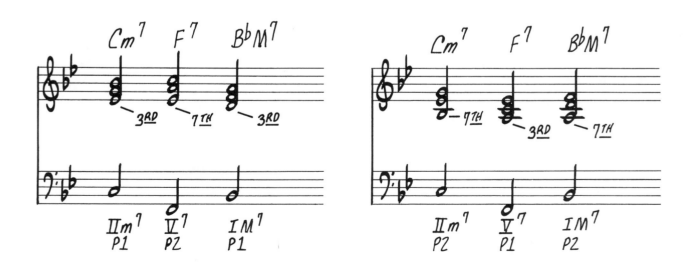

The chords are fingered the same in all keys.

4: THE NINTH CHORDS

The NINTH note above the root may be added to the seventh chords. The ninth is played with the fifth finger in Position 1 and with the second finger in Position 2.

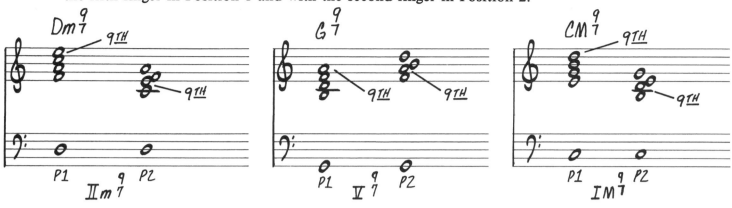

The ninth is added to the II V I chord progression.

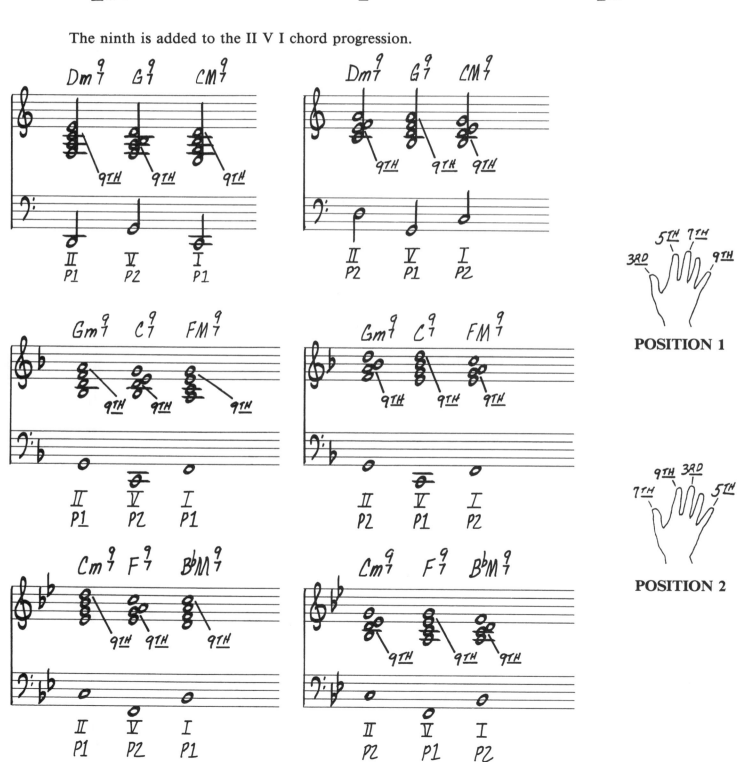

5: THE SIXTH AND THIRTEENTH CHORDS

The sixth and the thirteenth are the same tones:

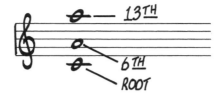

The sixth and thirteenth are added to different chord types and are therefore treated separately.

THE SIXTH CHORD

The 6th is added to major 7th chords and is played with the second finger in Position 1 and with the 5th finger in Position 2. The chord 5th is omitted. The root, 3rd and 7th must be included in all Position 1 and 2 voicings. The inclusion of the 5th is optional with some chords.

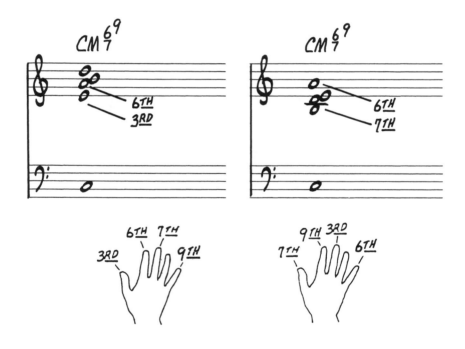

The 9th is usually included with the 6th.

THE THIRTEENTH CHORD

The 13th is added to dominant 7th chords and the 9th is included. The 5th is omitted from this voicing. The 13th is played by the second finger in Position 1 and by the 5th finger in Position 2.

The 6th and the 13th are added to the II V I chord progression.

6: SUMMARY OF UNALTERED CHORDS

All the unaltered chords have been discussed. Before going on to altered chords, review all the chord progressions in the keys of C, F and Bb. Not only memorize the chord progression but also memorize each chord out of the context of the progression. The following summaries should help to review.

The fingering chart illustrates which chord members are played by each finger. Altered chords will be fingered in the same manner.

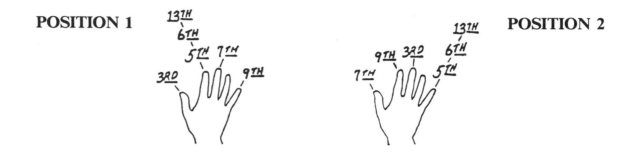

CHORD SUMMARY:

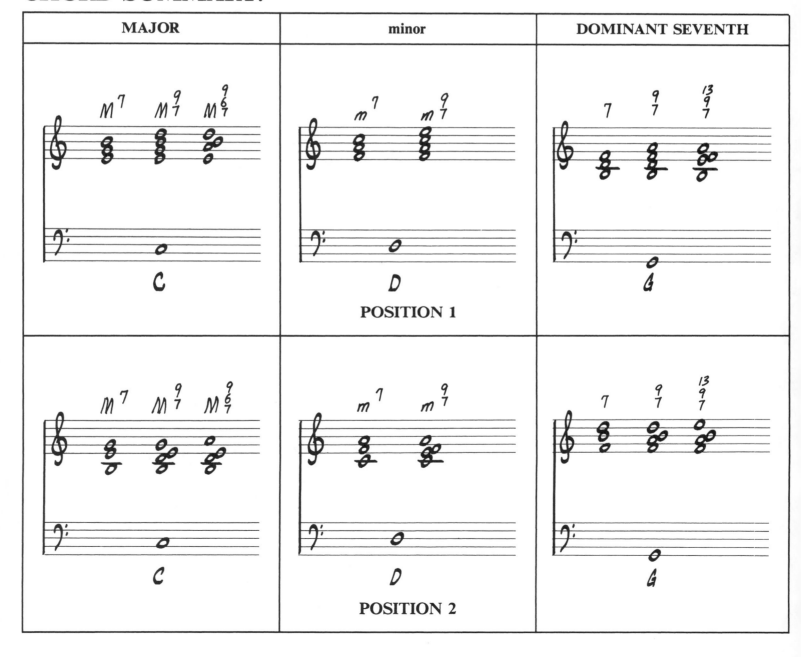

The following exercises review the II V I chord progression in the keys of C, F and B♭. Added notes occur at random. A bass line is added which includes chord roots and scale tones.

The next exercise illustrates the anticipated beat (syncopation) in the right hand part. The I chord is played one half a beat earlier and is tied into the first beat of the next measure.

Play the II V I exercises in the preceding chapters with a bass line.

Even with a limited chord vocabulary it is now possible to play some chord progressions to standard songs. Purchase sheet music such as Hal Leonard's *The Real Book* (volumes 1–3) from your local music store. Select songs that contain unaltered chords and are in the keys of C, F, or Bb. Chords that are unfamiliar may be found in Appendix A under basic voicing Position 1 or Position 2.

Decide on the chord position, memorize the chords and play the progressions with or without a bass line. Change major triads to M7 and minor triads to m7. Diminished chords may be found in Chapter 12. It may not be possible to play all of the chords. Most songs contain altered chords and chords which have not yet been discussed. However the experience and practice are invaluable at this point.

CHORD SYMBOLS IN FAKE BOOKS

The 7th is sometimes not indicated in chord symbols where notes above the seventh are added to the chord. For example:

CM^9 presumes the inclusion of the 7th $CM7^9$

Cm^9 presumes $Cm7^9$

$C13$ presumes $C7^{9^{13}}$

For additional chord symbol variations review the chart at the conclusion of Chapter 1.

If there is no chord symbol over a measure, use the chord from the preceding measure.

The standard twelve measure blues chord progression also provides excellent practice.

BLUES IN C

*THE ULTIMATE FAKE BOOK   Published by Hal Leonard

Work out the following chord progression. Use the Blues in C as a guide. The slashes in the measures below indicate the beats. Look up the G♭7^9 and the E7^9 chords in Appendix A. The CD tracks offer both slow and fast versions, and feature bass and drumset. Play along with this rhythm section on the CD.

BLUES IN F

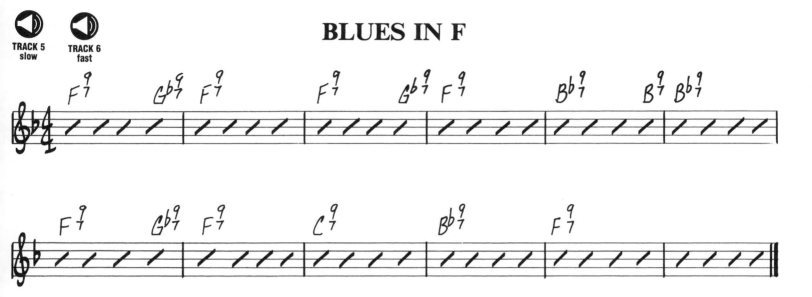

Play the chord progressions to the following songs which may be found in the *The Real Book*, Volume 1 (Hal Leonard Corporation).

West Coast Blues: *The Real Book* v. 1, page 436.

Ring Dem Bells: *The Real Book* v. 1, page 341.

Paper Doll: *The Real Book* v. 1, page 319.

Blue Monk: *The Real Book* v. 1, page 52.

The Blue Room: *The Real Book* v. 1, page 53.

7: THE ALTERED FIFTH AND ELEVENTH CHORDS

Chords may contain notes which are raised or lowered one half a step. Chords with chromatic alterations are called altered chords.

SYMBOLS FOR ALTERED CHORDS			
+ or ♯	raised	augmented	sharp
- or ♭	lowered	flatted	

Examples:
G7 -5
G7 ♭5   "flatted fifth"   "lowered fifth"

G7 +5   "sharp fifth"   "raised fifth"
G7 ♯5   "augmented fifth"

Altered notes usually appear in dominant seventh chords.

♭5th   +11th

The flatted fifth and the augmented eleventh are the same tone:

Both chords are virtually the same. The +11 symbol occasionally appears but the ♭5 is the more common designation.

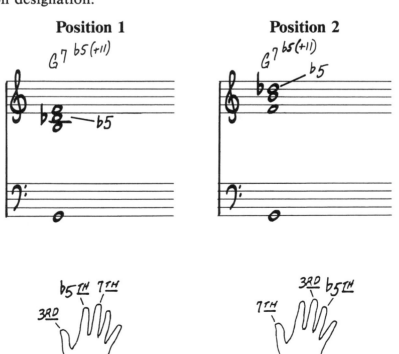

Position 1   **Position 2**

♯5th

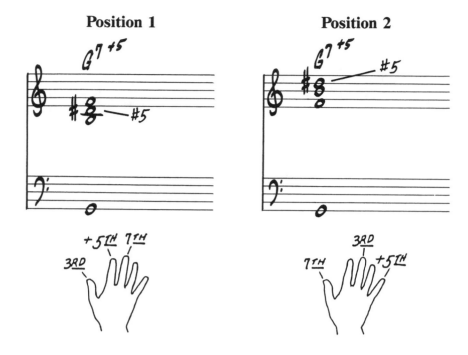

II V I chord progression including the ♯5th with the V chord:

8: THE ALTERED NINTH CHORDS

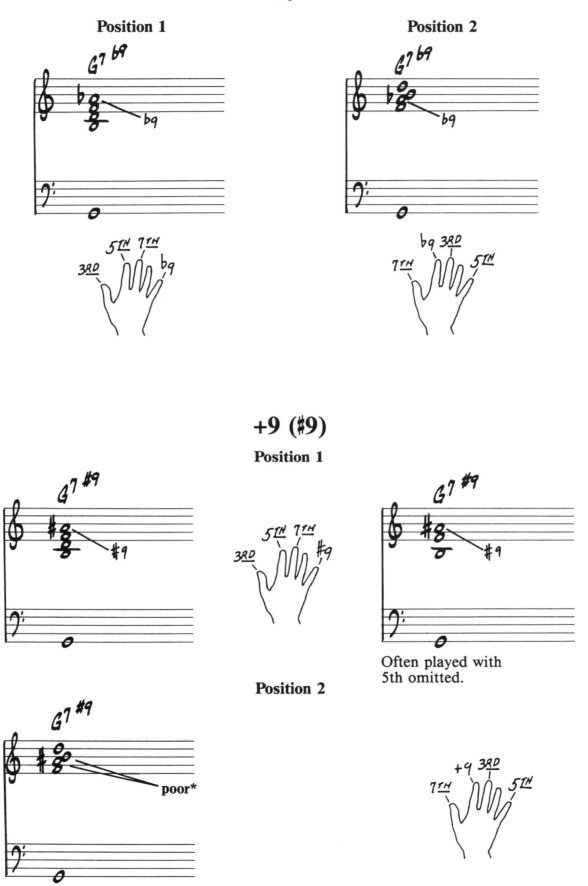

*Position 2 is somewhat dissonant as the ♯9 (A♯) and the 3rd (B) are one half step apart. An alternate voicing will be discussed in another chapter.

Exercises with the ♭9th.

Exercises with the ♯9th.

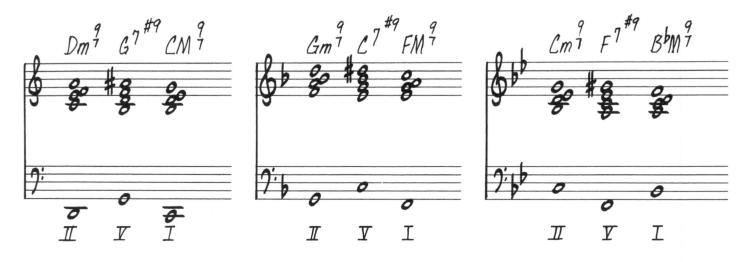

9: COMBINATION CHORDS

There are several combinations of altered and unaltered notes which may appear within the same chord. A thorough understanding of the preceding chapters is essential before attempting these more complicated chord structures.

Review the composite fingering chart.

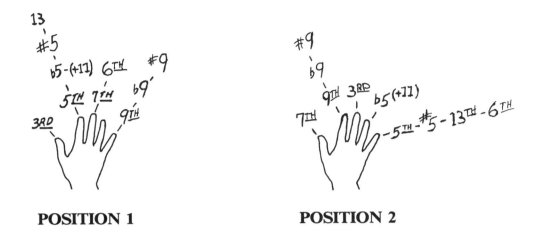

POSITION 1   POSITION 2

The altered notes are played by the second and fifth fingers in Position 1 and 2. The only exception is the ♭5 in Position 2. The first and third fingers remain on the 3rd and 7th. Notice that the relationship between the chord member and the fingering is reversed from Position 1 to Position 2.

The V chords for the keys of C, F and B♭ serve as examples.

G7 Position 1

Position 2

24

C7   Position 1

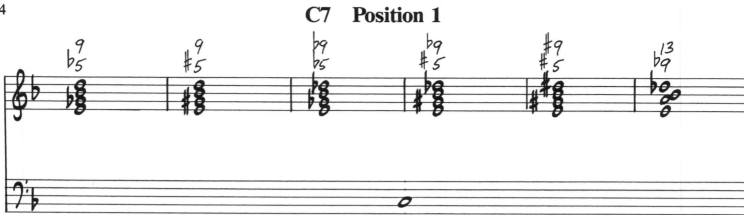

Position 2

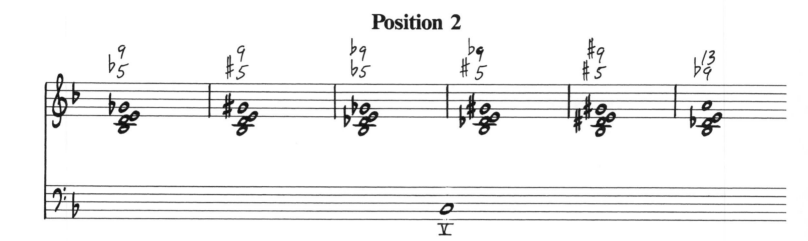

F7 Position 1

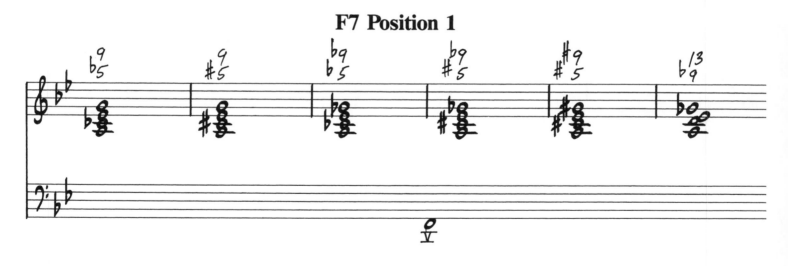

Position 2

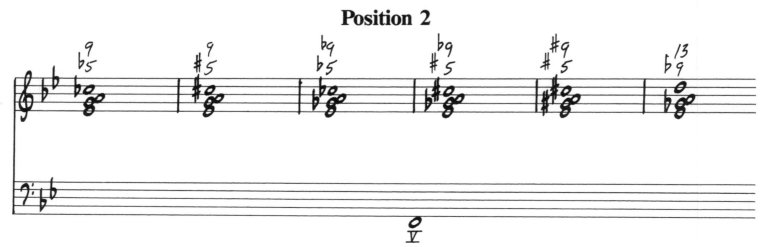

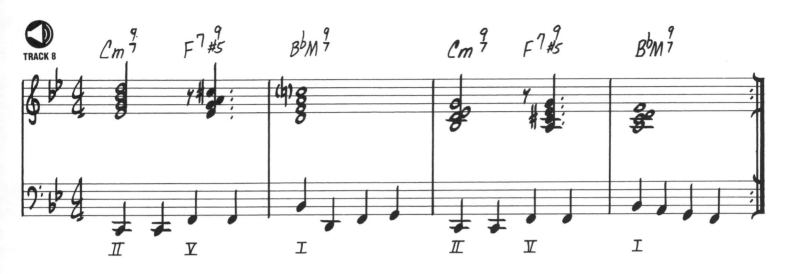

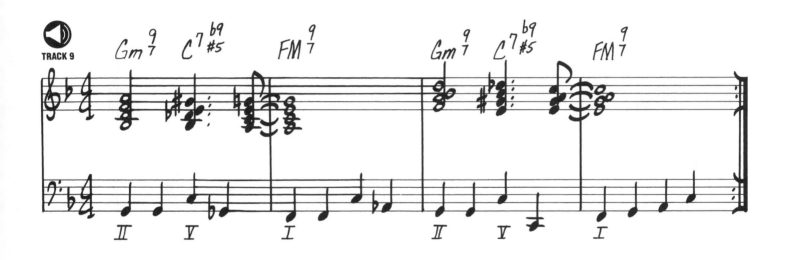

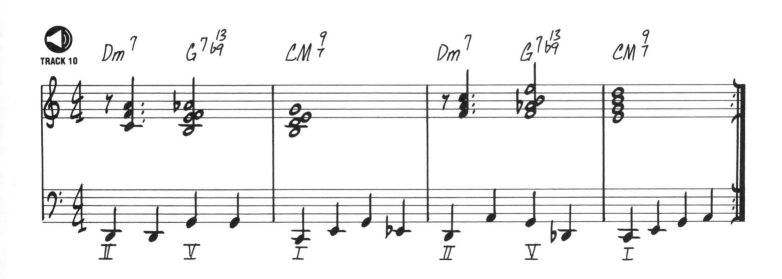

10: II V I IN MINOR

The I chord is a m7 add 9th or a m6 add 9th.

Position 1   **Position 2**

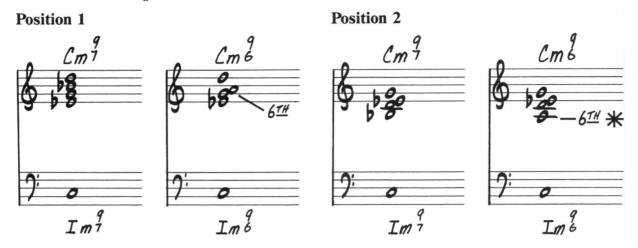

*The m6 in Position 2 is the one exception to the thumb rule. To play this chord, the thumb must move from its place on the 7th down one half a step to the 6th.

The V7 chord is an altered dominant seventh.

The II chord is a minor seventh chord with a flatted 5th (m7-⁵). When the ninth is added it is flatted.

Position 1   **Position 2**

The m7-⁵ is sometimes designated a half diminished 7th chord.
Symbol: ∅

11: VARIATION VOICINGS

A variation on the basic voicings is available for both Position 1 and 2. The right hand fingerings remain the same.

In Position 1 the 7th is removed from the right hand and placed in the left hand seven notes above the root.

In Position 2 the 3rd is omitted from the right hand and added to the left hand three notes above the root.

There are two advantages in having one less note in the right hand.

1. The cluttered sound of the raised 9th in Position 2 is eliminated.

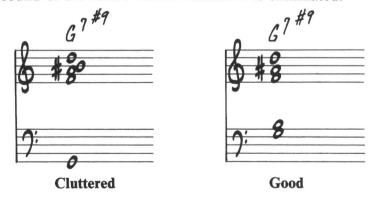

2. Additional notes may be included in the chord.

The 13th is played with the third finger in Pos. 1. All other fingerings remain the same.

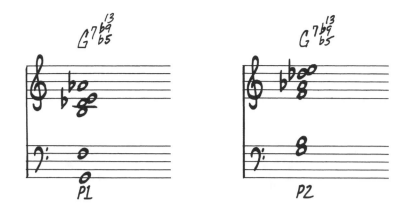

It is impractical to play a moving bass line accompaniment with this voicing.

The left hand should be played in a register that will sound well. Generally the top note of the left hand part will be within an octave of the bottom note in the right hand.

12: TRIADS AND DIMINISHED 7th CHORDS

Triads are not often used in jazz and for that reason have not been included in the appendix. Discussion here is for general information rather than for practical application. An acceptable voicing of triads would place the root in the left hand and any inversion of the triad in the right hand.

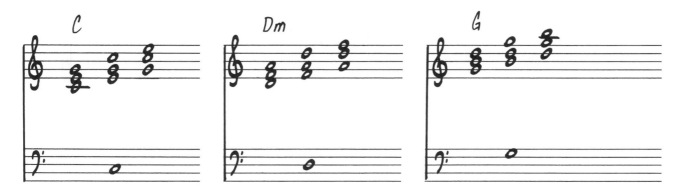

In the II V I progression choose an inversion which allows the same finger to play the note common to both chords. The common tones are filled in for the examples below:

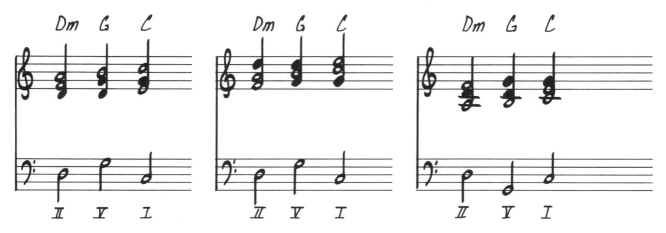

The DIMINISHED 7th chord (o, Dim. or dim.7) is a difficult chord to analyze. There are three different diminished 7th chords each containing four notes.

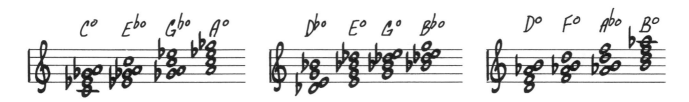

Any chord member may appear in the left hand as the root and any inversion may be played in the right hand.

A more contemporary sound is achieved by replacing the top note in any inversion with the note one whole step above. The added note may never be used as the root.

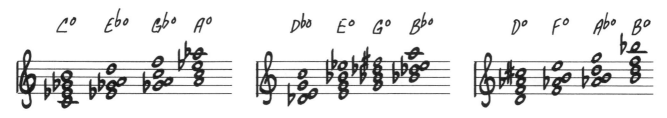

13: "COMPING"

"Comping" is the jazz vernacular for accompanying. The pianist often improvises an accompaniment based on the chord progression. A stage band piano part is sometimes improvised, especially during jazz solo passages. The pianist always improvises in a small group.

In the absence of a bass player, the pianist should provide an accompaniment similar to the II V I exercises which include a bass line. A typical bass line will consist of roots, fifths, chord tones and scale passages.

ROOTS AND FIFTHS

SCALES AND CHORD TONES

The roots may be approached from one half step above.

"Comping" in the key of F:

TRACK 11

Review the exercises which contain bass lines.

When a bass player is part of the group, the pianist must not improvise a bass line which would conflict with the bass part. Instead, play various rhythm patterns with both hands. The basic and variation voicings may be used for this purpose.

BASIC VOICING

The addition of the VI7 chord after the I chord provides a better "lead back" to the IIm7 chord.

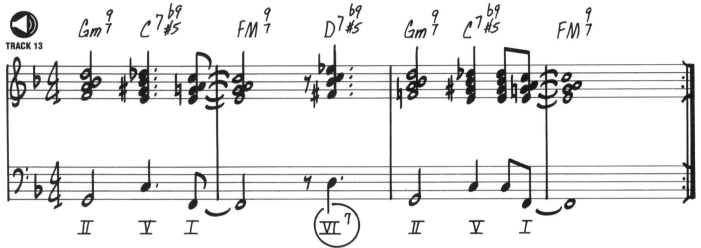

VARIATION VOICING

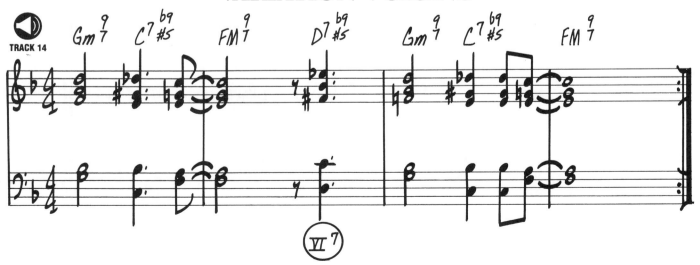

A third type of chord voicing is also possible. The left hand plays the notes normally played by the right hand in Positions 1 and 2. Often the fifth is omitted. The right hand may play any number of notes which compliment the chord. The possibilities here are many. Therefore, this voicing is only presented as a point of information and a detailed analysis is beyond the scope of this book. This subject is dealt with more extensively in advanced books on chord voicing.

A simple blues chord progression demonstrates the third type of voicing.

When improvising an accompaniment with a stage band LISTEN to the arrangement. Do not interfere with the figures played by the band. Some rhythmic patterns (or kicks) must be played with the sections of the band. These parts must be read note for note. When "comping" for a soloist play a simple rhythmic pattern . . . lay back and try to compliment the soloist and provide an accurate chord background. LISTENING is the key. LISTEN to recordings of small jazz groups as they provide the best examples of "comping."

Purchase sheet music or "FAKE" books from your local music dealer. Use the chord progressions written above the melody line and develop your own accompaniments.

Select a song, decide on the type of chord voicing (basic or variation). Find the chords in Appendix A and memorize the voicings. If you play a bass line, use roots, fifths and other chord tones. Roots may occasionally be approached from one half step above.

The example below is a chord progression to a slow ballad. The slashes in the measures indicate the beats.

BASIC VOICING

VARIATION VOICING

Develop accompaniments from the two examples below. Play your new accompaniments along with the CD.

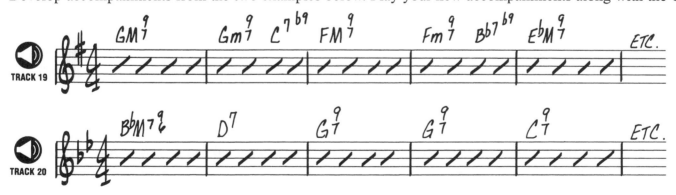

"Fake" books do not always indicate four note chords or chords with added and/or altered notes. Therefore the pianist must make these additions on his own in order to achieve a full and idiomatic jazz sound. Major and minor triads become Major seventh and minor seventh chords with or without added notes. Augmented triads are played as dominant 7th chords with the raised fifth. Dominant seventh chords may contain added and altered notes when appropriate.

Develop accompaniments for the following songs which may be found in Hal Leonard's *The Real Book* Volume 1.

How High The Moon: *The Real Book* v. 1, page 180.

Cherokee (Indian Love Song): *The Real Book* v. 1, page 77.

Darn That Dream: *The Real Book* v. 1, page 99.

Desafinado: *The Real Book* v. 1, page 108.

14: MELODY PLAYING

The basic and variation chord voicings may be adapted to melody playing.

Over an octave of potential melody notes may be reached by combining Positions 1 and 2.

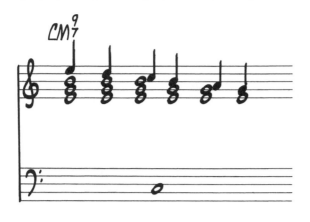

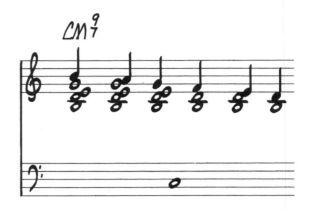

POSITION 1　　　　　　　　　　　**POSITION 2**

Some overlapping occurs. In instances where there are two choices either position will suffice. It does not matter that with some melody notes several chord members are absent. Play the melody with the fourth or fifth fingers and sustain the remaining chord tones.

When the melody contains eighth notes, the chord tones included in the melody are not sustained. Play a full chord on notes of longer duration.

When there are wide skips in the melody, it is not always possible to go from a Position 1 to a Position 2 chord for root movement of a fourth or fifth.

Two steps are required in order to play a melody in this style.

STEP 1: Select the chord position (voicing) which best suits the melody note. (It is sometimes possible to use either position.) Practice these positions before adding the melody.

STEP 2: Add the melody to the top of the voicing and sustain the remaining chord members.

Melody "A" is four measures. Each four measure example is written under the other and the measures are numbered for analyzation.

MELODY "A"

Example 4 suggests optional voicings for measures one and three. In measure one use Position 1 and stretch. More chord tones are possible with this voicing. In measure three, Position 1 for the first chord requires less of a skip moving to the next chord. However, there are fewer chord tones to sustain. In the original version there is a skip when moving from the first to the second chord but the result is a fuller sound because more chord tones are present in the first chord.

Melody "A" harmonized with the variation voicing:

An optional voicing for the first chord in measure one:

A. This voicing eliminates the stretch. However there are three Position 2 voicings in a row because of the wide range of the melody.

B. Avoid this by using Position 1 for the first chord in measure two.

MELODY "B"

The melody is eight measures in length and is harmonized with a more complicated chord progression. The same format is followed.

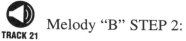

Melody "B" STEP 2:

Below is an optional version for measures two and four. Position 1 is possible in both instances with a stretch. There are more chord tones present in this version.

This style is best suited to solo playing and slow ballads.

Another style of playing the melody is especially effective with a rhythm section. The right hand plays the melody. The left hand plays the chord tones formerly played by the right hand in the basic voicing. Some chords will not sound complete as there are no roots. The bass player will convey the root movement.

MELODY "A" in this style:

STEP 1:   Find the chords in Appendix A and select the chord voicing (position).

STEP 2:   Transfer the right hand notes in the voicing to the left hand. The fingerings for the left hand chords will usually be 5-3-2-1.

STEP 3:   Play the chords with the left hand and the melody with the right hand.

Select melodies from the "FAKE" book, follow the three steps above and practice this style of melody playing.

Below are two suggested songs from Hal Leonard's *The Real Book* Volumes 1 and 2.

Imagination: *The Real Book* v. 2, page 195.
Long Ago (And Far Away): *The Real Book* v. 1, page 251.

Melody "C" is a four measure jazz line. Notice how the left hand emphasizes some of the rhythmic figures in the right hand.

MELODY "C"

MELODY "D"

In this style the melody is played in octaves one octave higher than written. The left hand chords duplicate the rhythm of the melody.

The many variations on these styles of melody playing are too numerous to be covered in this book. Careful practice of the examples will provide a basic foundation on which to build.

Practice melodies from the "FAKE" book in the various styles presented in this chapter.

GUIDE TO APPENDIX A

MAJOR CHORDS

MINOR CHORDS

DOMINANT SEVENTH CHORDS

APPENDIX A

MAJOR SEVENTH   Symbol: M, Maj.7, △

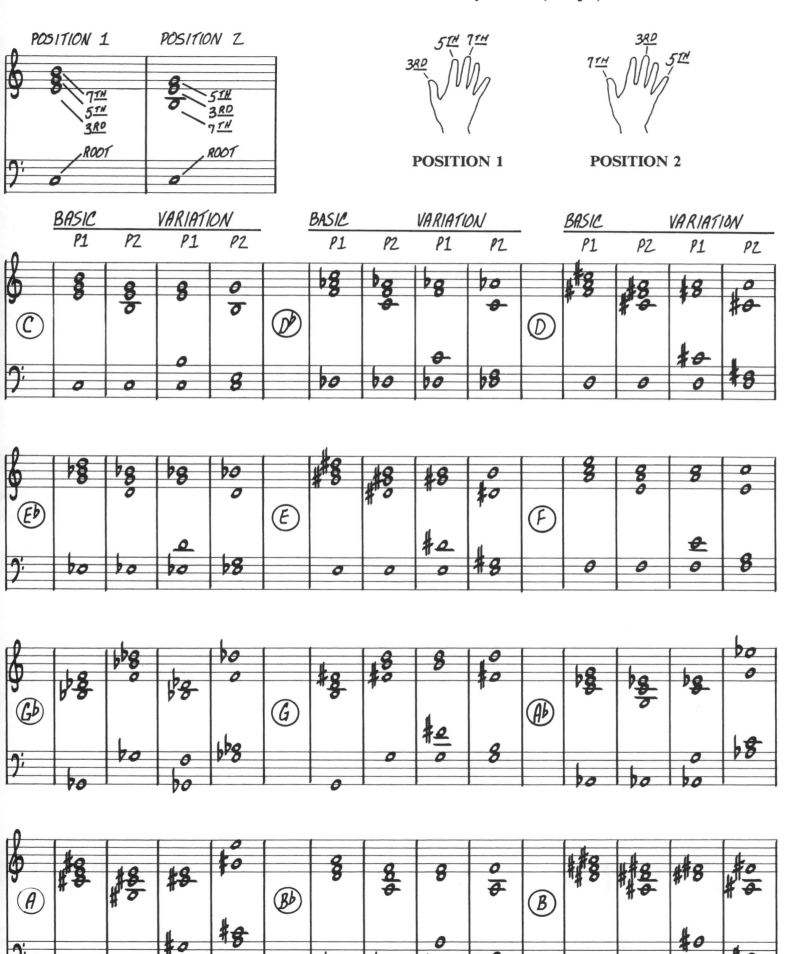

APPENDIX A

MAJOR 7th and 9th

Symbol: M7⁹ M9

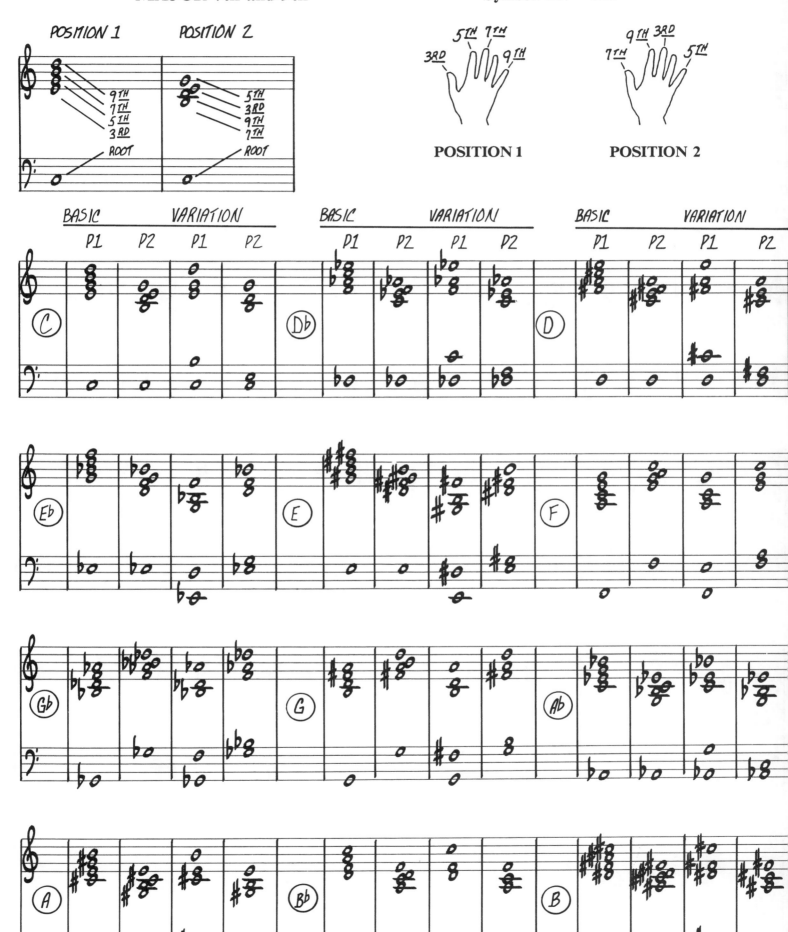

APPENDIX A

MAJOR 7th add 6th and 9th

Symbol: M76⁹ M6⁹

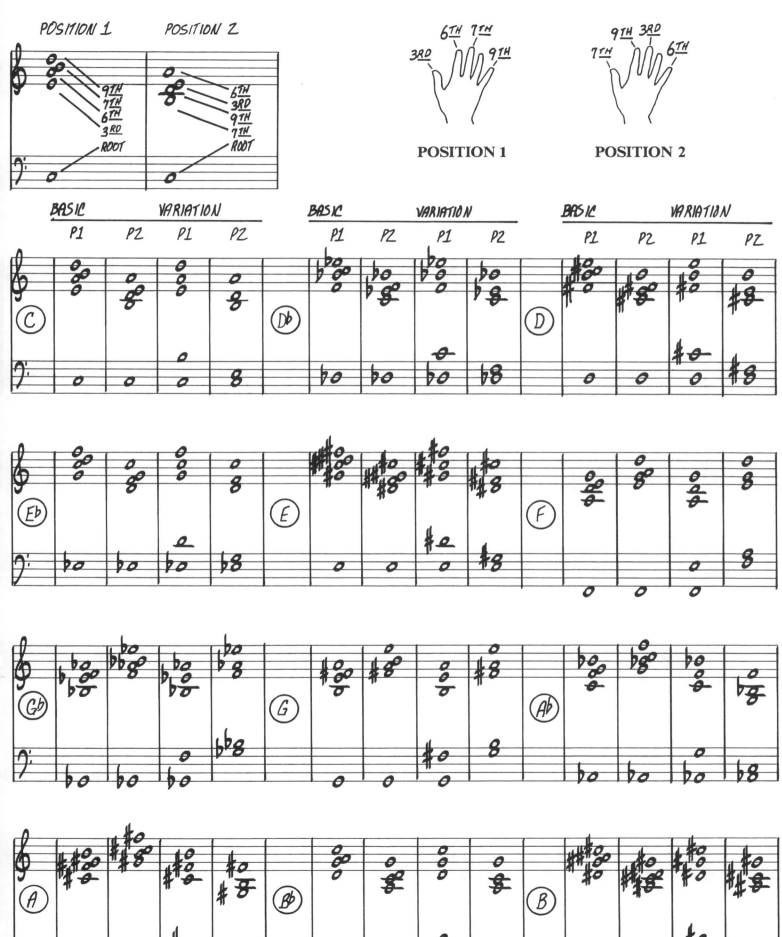

APPENDIX A

minor 7th

Symbol: m7   -7

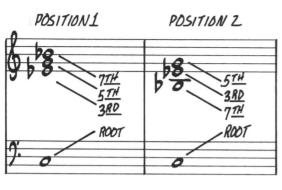

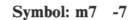

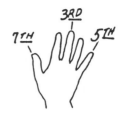

POSITION 1   POSITION 2

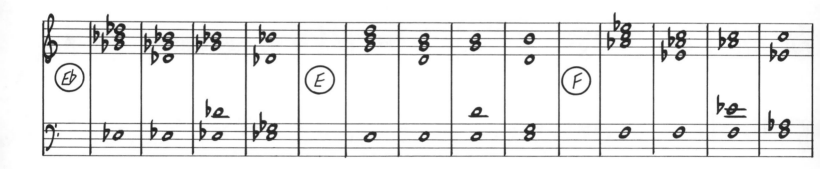

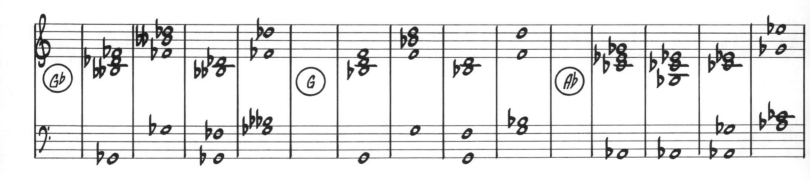

APPENDIX A

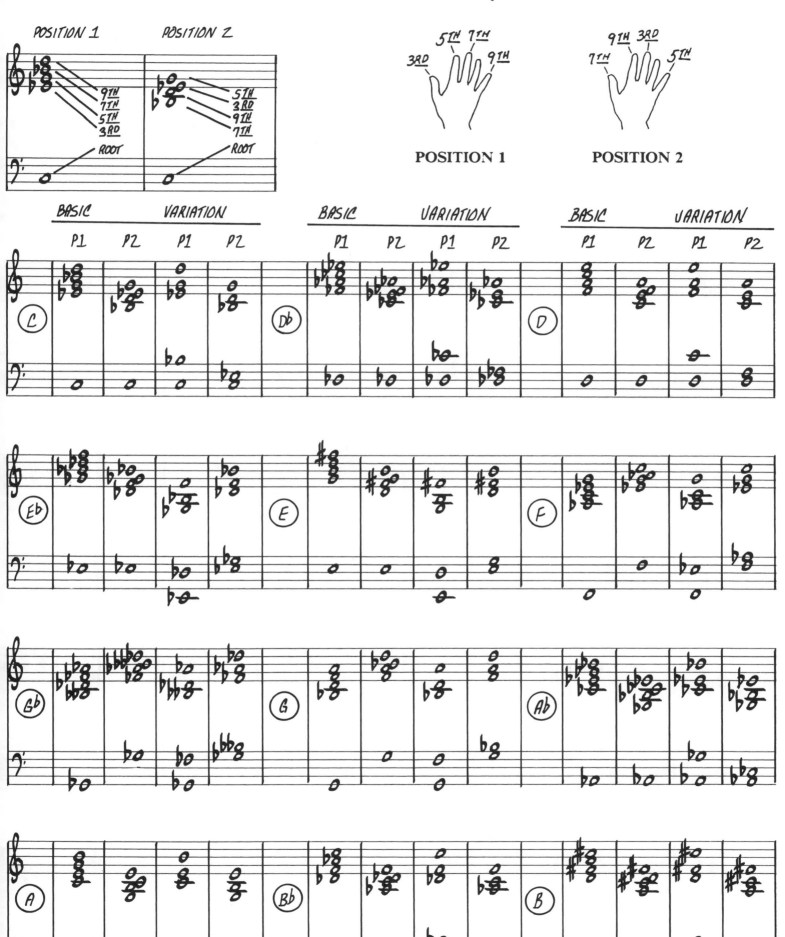

APPENDIX A

MINOR SIXTH ADD NINTH (I chord in minor key)   Symbol: m6⁹

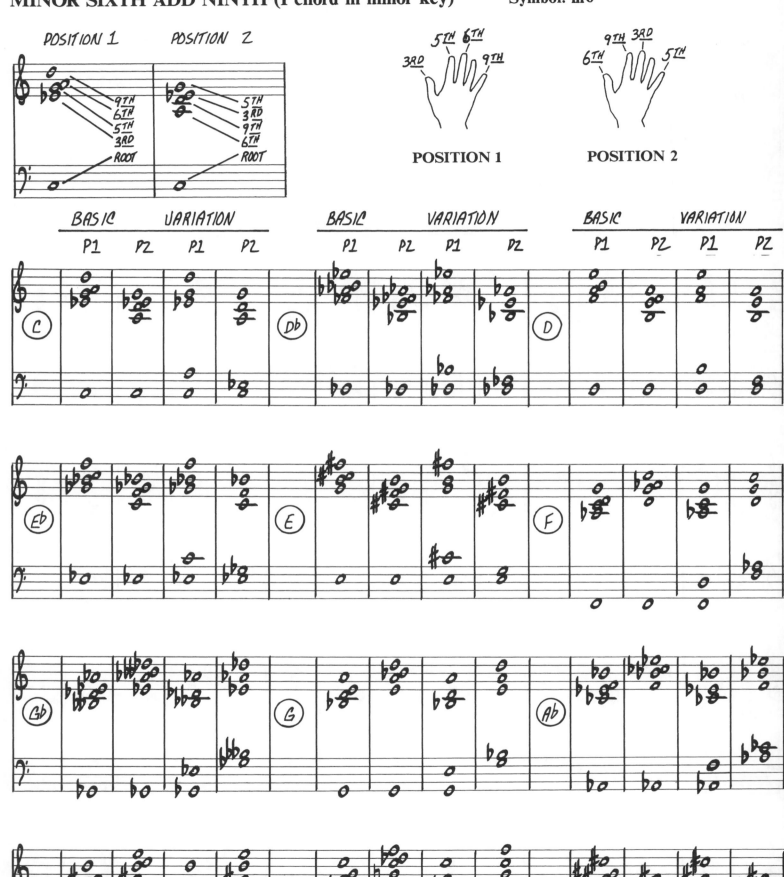

APPENDIX A

MINOR 7th flat 5th **Symbol: m7-5 -7b5°**

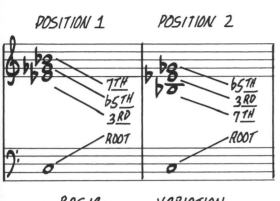

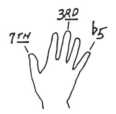

POSITION 1 **POSITION 2**

APPENDIX A

DOMINANT SEVENTH

Symbol: 7

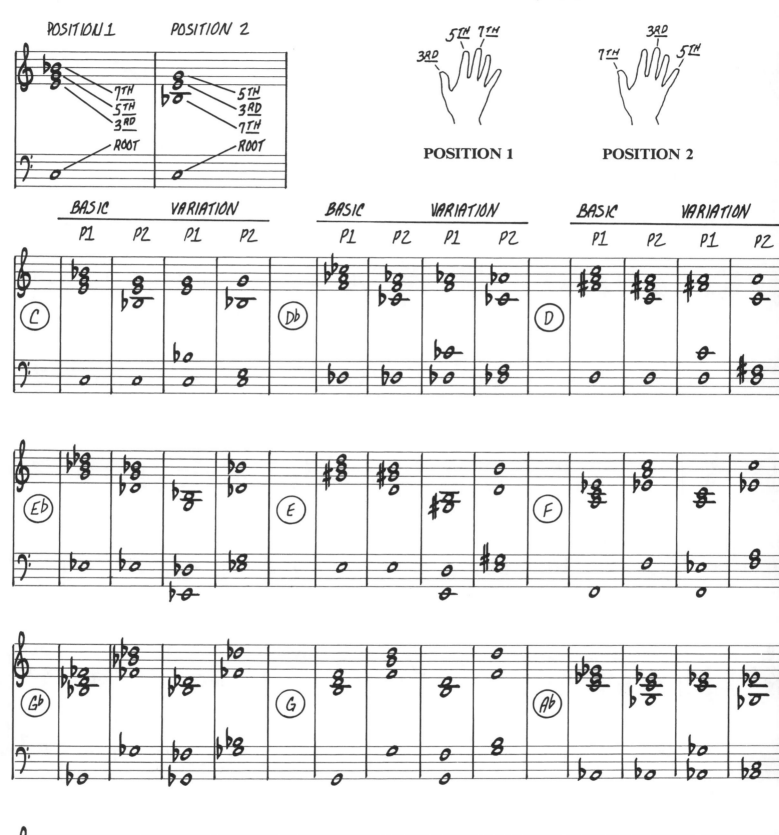

APPENDIX A

DOMINANT 7th ADD 9th Symbol: 7♭9

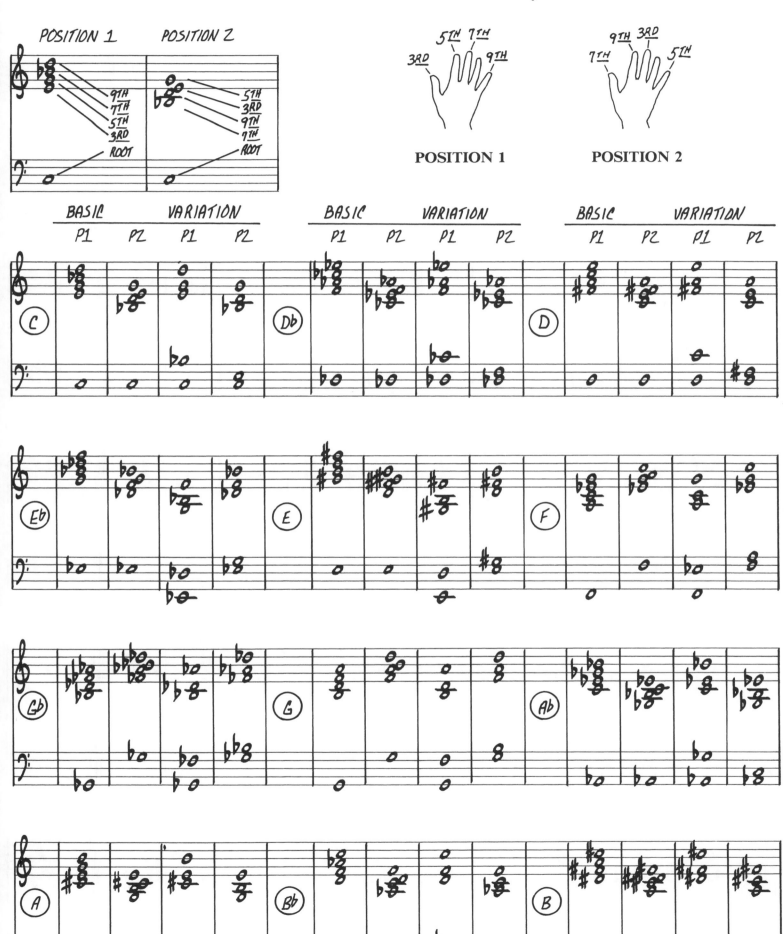

APPENDIX A

DOMINANT 7th add 9th and 13th

Symbol: $7^{9^{13}}$ 13

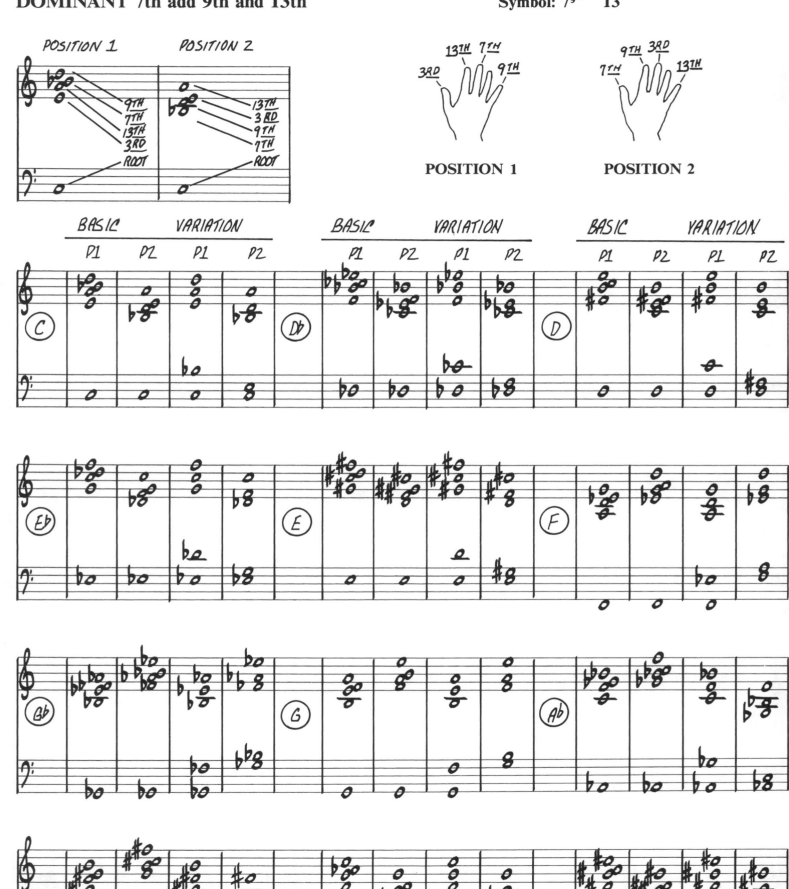

APPENDIX A

DOMINANT SEVENTH FLAT FIFTH (aug. 11)   Symbol: 7(♭5) +11

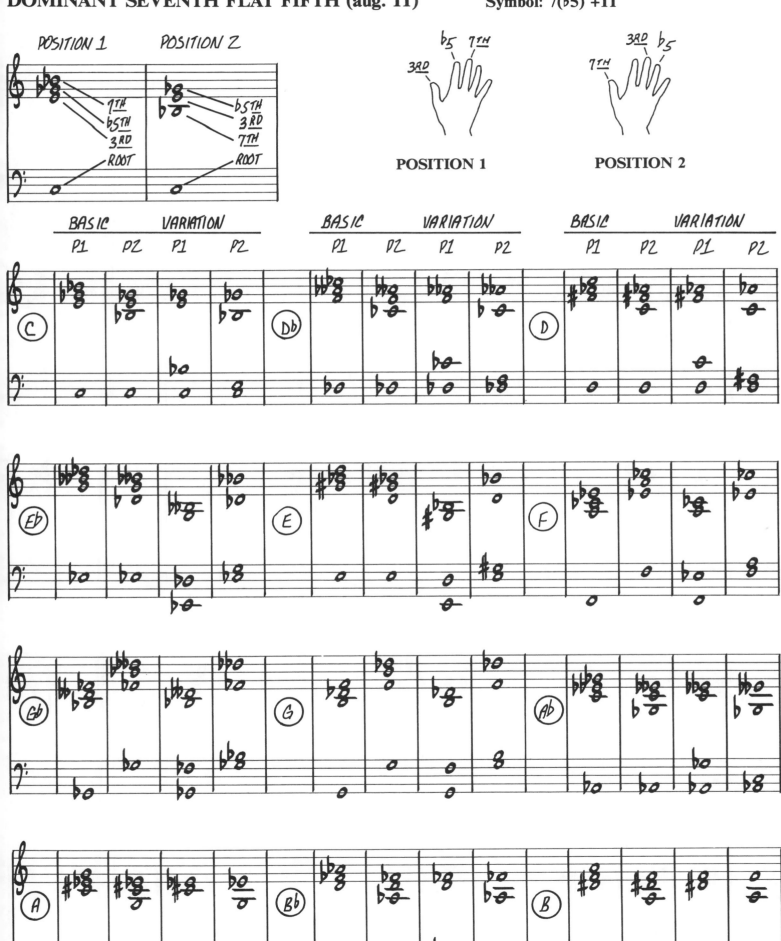

APPENDIX A

DOMINANT SEVENTH SHARP FIFTH

Symbol: 7(#5) 7+5 +

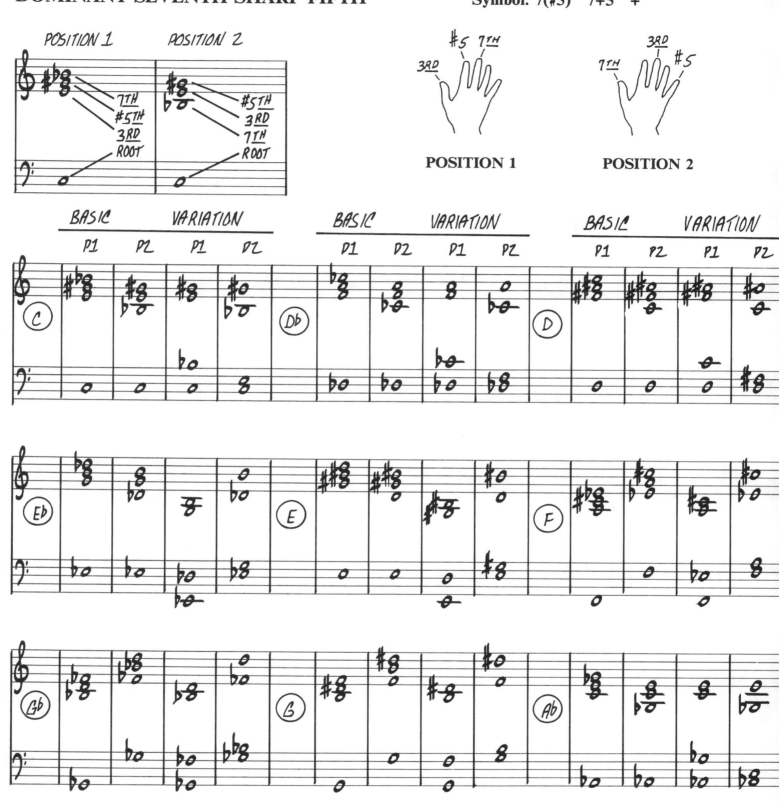

APPENDIX A

DOMINANT SEVENTH FLAT FIFTH (augmented 11) add 9th   Symbol: 7⁹(♭5)+11

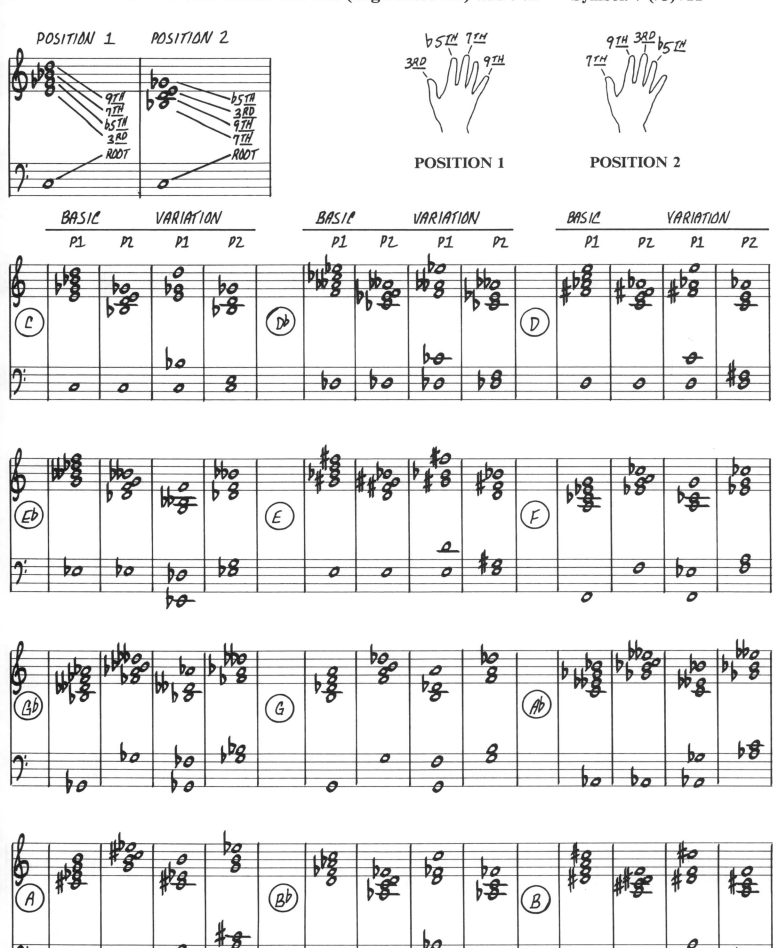

APPENDIX A

DOMINANT 7th   sharp 5th add 9th

Symbol: $+5 \atop 9$ $\#5 \atop 9$

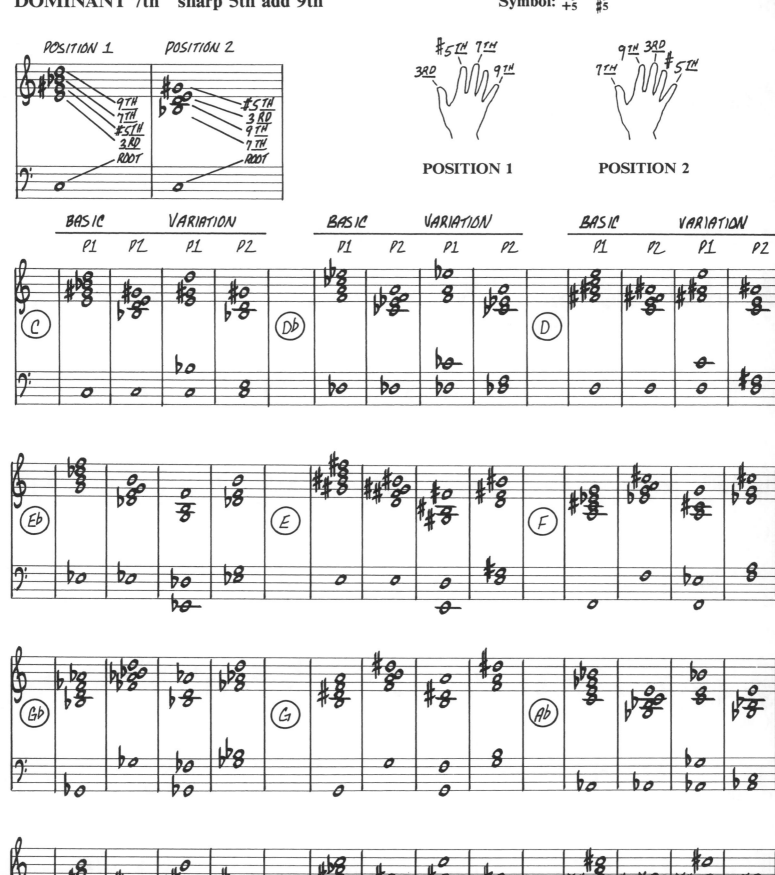

APPENDIX A

DOMINANT 7th flat 9th   Symbol: $7^{\flat 9}$

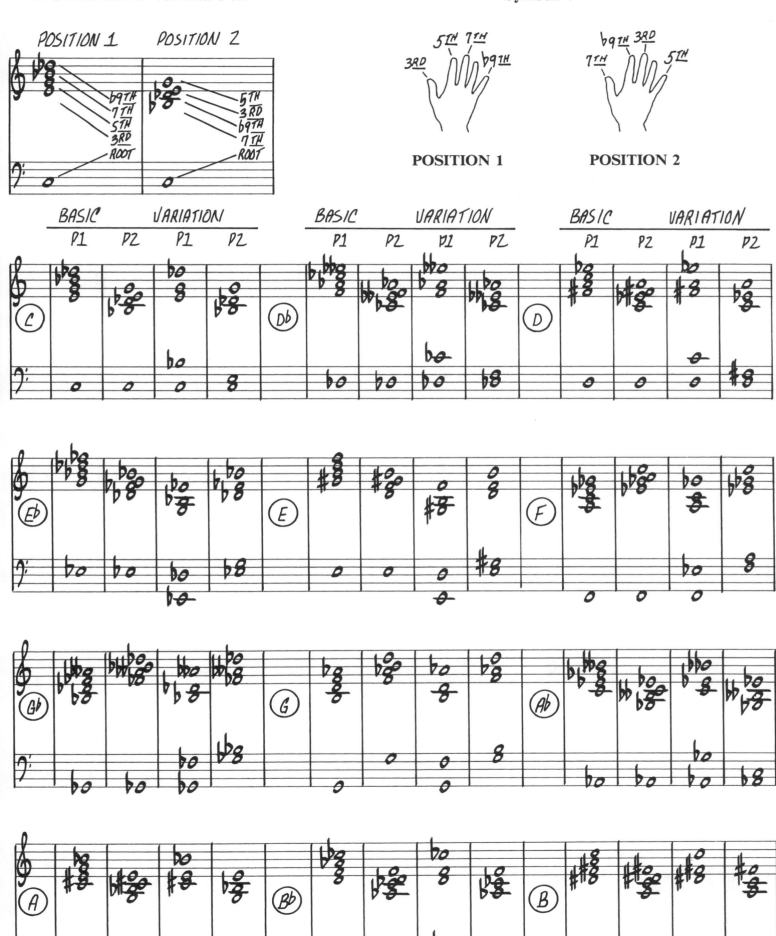

APPENDIX A

DOMINANT 7th sharp 9th   Symbol: 7^{+9} 7$^{\#9}$

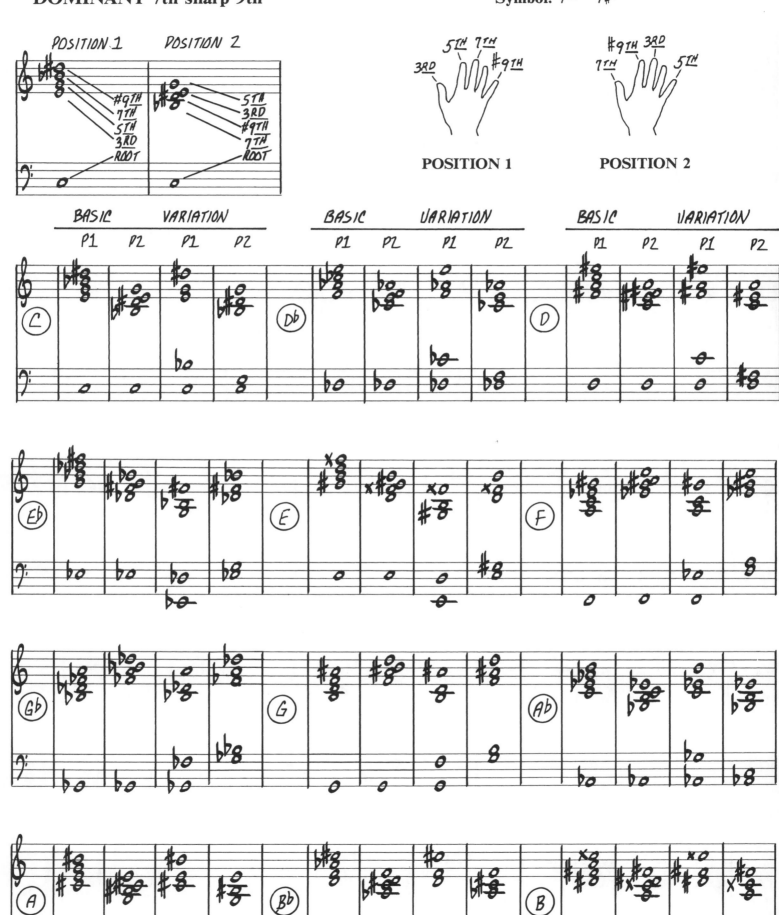

APPENDIX A

DOMINANT SEVENTH SHARP FIFTH SHARP NINTH

Symbol: 7 #5#9

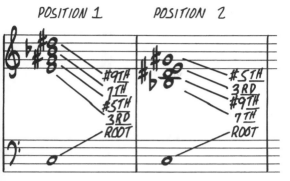

POSITION 1　　　　**POSITION 2**

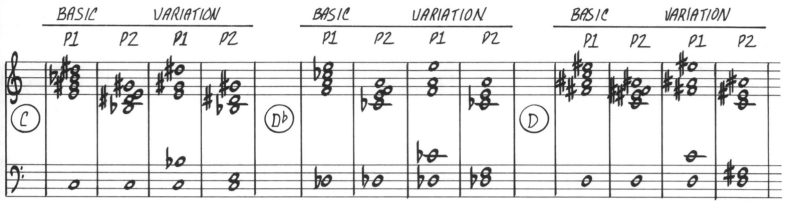

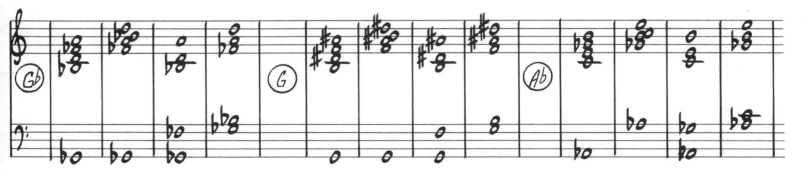

APPENDIX A

DOMINANT SEVENTH FLAT FIFTH   FLAT NINTH

Symbol: b9 (b5)

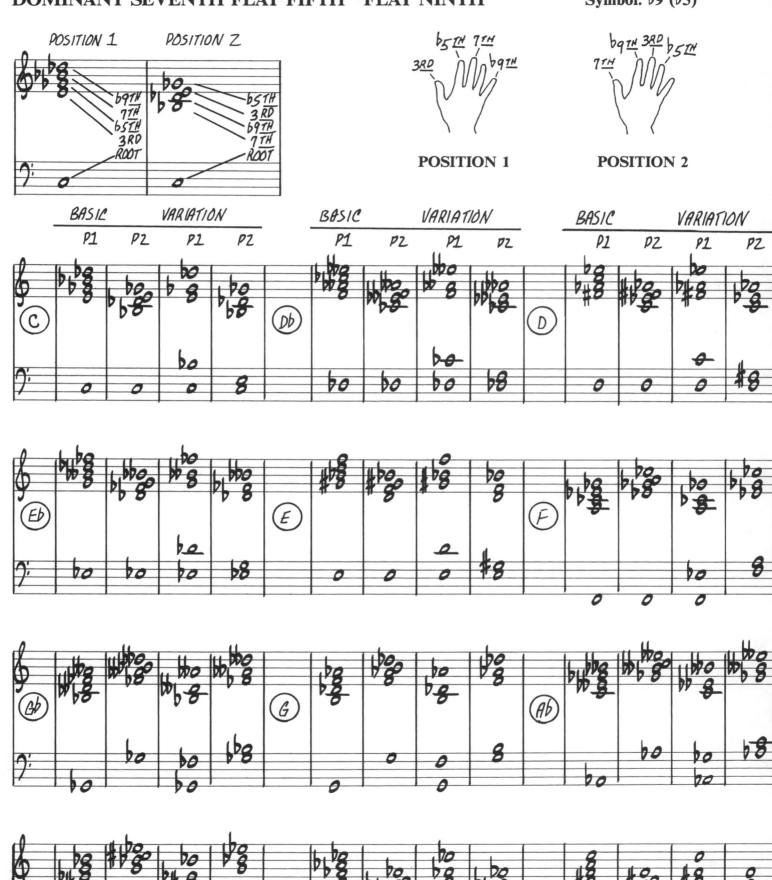

DOMINANT 7th sharp 5   flat 9

Symbol: 7+5⁻⁹

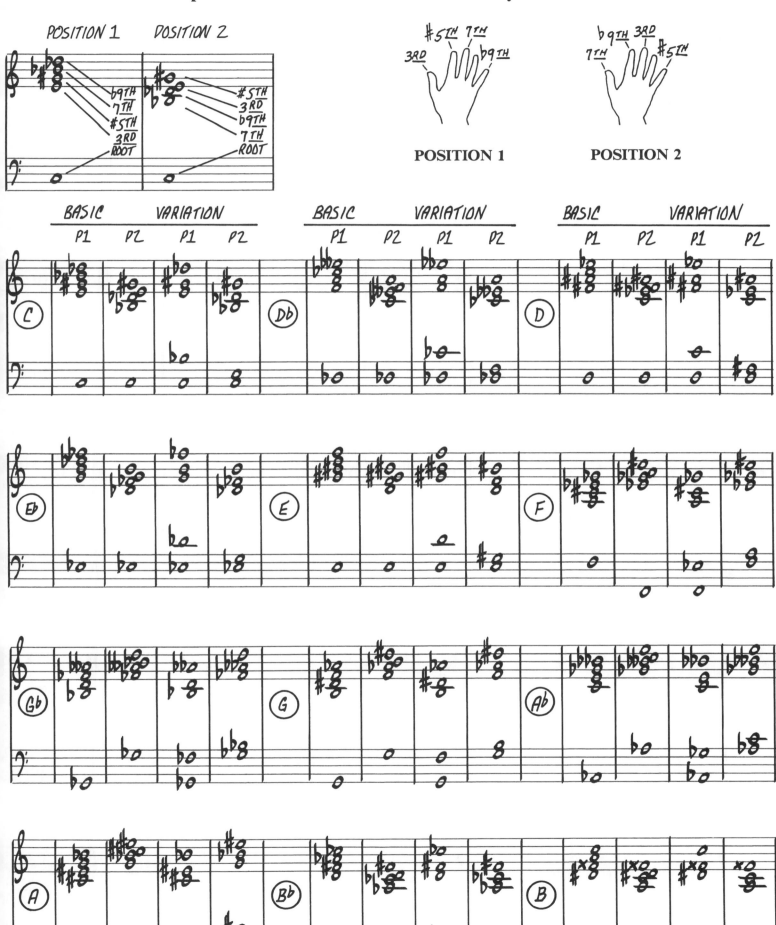

APPENDIX A

DOMINANT 7th add flat 9th add 13th   Symbol: 7-9¹³   7♭9¹³

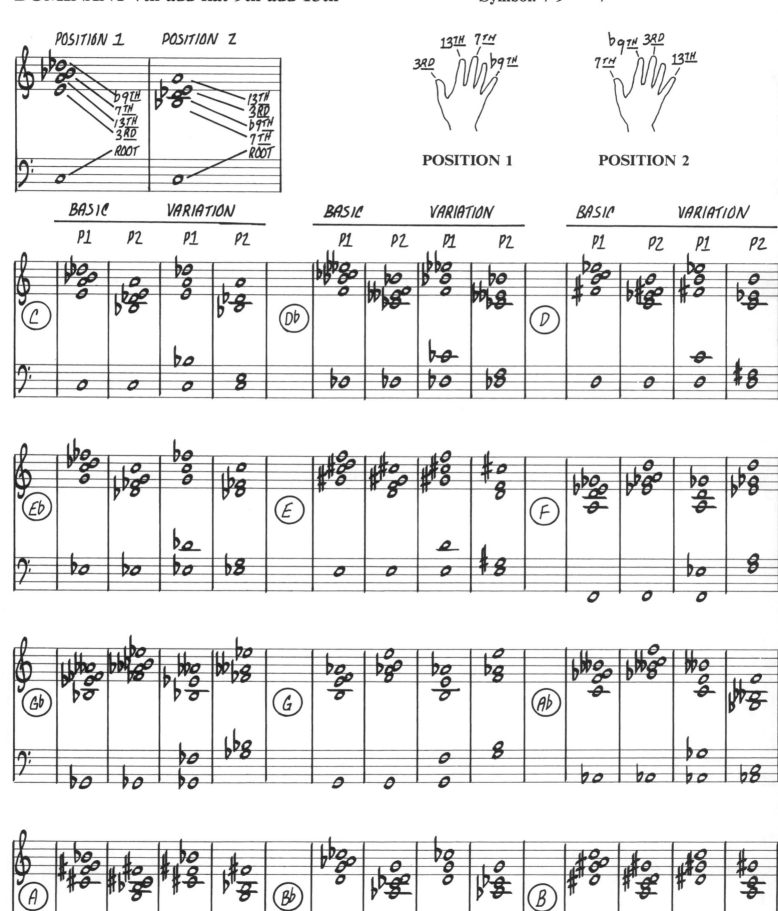

60

APPENDIX B
II V I ALL MAJOR KEYS

APPENDIX B
II V I ALL MAJOR KEYS

Altered notes may be added to the V chords in this section.

APPENDIX C
II V I ALL MINOR KEYS

64

APPENDIX C
II   V   I   ALL MINOR KEYS

APPENDIX D
COMMON CHORD PROGRESSIONS WITH ALTERED CHORDS

66

APPENDIX D
COMMON CHORD PROGRESSION WITH ALTERED CHORDS

APPENDIX D
COMMON CHORD PROGRESSIONS WITH ALTERED CHORDS

The Keyboard Play-Along series will help you quickly and easily play your favorite songs as played by your favorite artists. Just follow the music in the book, listen to the CD to hear how the keyboard should sound, and then play along using the separate backing tracks. The melody and lyrics are also included in the book in case you want to sing, or simply to help you follow along. The audio CD is playable on any CD player. For PC and Mac users, the CD is enhanced so you can adjust the recording to any tempo without changing pitch! Each book/CD pack in this series features eight great songs.

1. POP/ROCK HITS

Against All Odds (Take a Look at Me Now) (Phil Collins) • Deacon Blues (Steely Dan) • (Everything I Do) I Do It for You (Bryan Adams) • Hard to Say I'm Sorry (Chicago) • Kiss on My List (Hall & Oates) • My Life (Billy Joel) • Walking in Memphis (Marc Cohn) • What a Fool Believes (The Doobie Brothers).
00699875 Keyboard Transcriptions.......................................$14.95

2. SOFT ROCK

Don't Know Much (Aaron Neville) • Glory of Love (Peter Cetera) • I Write the Songs (Barry Manilow) • It's Too Late (Carole King) • Just Once (James Ingram) • Making Love Out of Nothing at All (Air Supply) • We've Only Just Begun (Carpenters) • You Are the Sunshine of My Life (Stevie Wonder).
00699876 Keyboard Transcriptions.......................................$12.95

3. CLASSIC ROCK

Against the Wind (Bob Seger) • Come Sail Away (Styx) • Don't Do Me like That (Tom Petty and the Heartbreakers) • Jessica (Allman Brothers) • Say You Love Me (Fleetwood Mac) • Takin' Care of Business (Bachman-Turner Overdrive) • Werewolves of London (Warren Zevon) • You're My Best Friend (Queen).
00699877 Keyboard Transcriptions.......................................$14.95

4. CONTEMPORARY ROCK

Angel (Sarah McLachlan) • Beautiful (Christina Aguilera) • Because of You (Kelly Clarkson) • Don't Know Why (Norah Jones) • Fallin' (Alicia Keys) • Listen to Your Heart (D.H.T.) • A Thousand Miles (Vanessa Carlton) • Unfaithful (Rihanna).
00699878 Keyboard Transcriptions.......................................$12.95

5. ROCK HITS

Back at One (Brian McKnight) • Brick (Ben Folds) • Clocks (Coldplay) • Drops of Jupiter (Tell Me) (Train) • Home (Michael Buble) • 100 Years (Five for Fighting) • This Love (Maroon 5) • You're Beautiful (James Blunt)
00699879 Keyboard Transcriptions.......................................$14.95

6. ROCK BALLADS

Bridge over Troubled Water (Simon & Garfunkel) • Easy (Commodores) • Hey Jude (Beatles) • Imagine (John Lennon) • Maybe I'm Amazed (Paul McCartney) • A Whiter Shade of Pale (Procol Harum) • You Are So Beautiful (Joe Cocker) • Your Song (Elton John).
00699880 Keyboard Transcriptions.......................................$14.95

More Volumes Coming Soon, Including:
Vol. 7 Rock Classics

Prices, contents, and availability subject to change without notice.

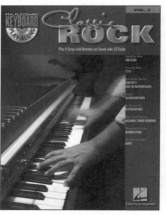

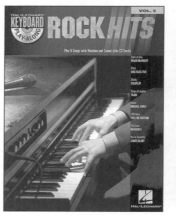

FOR MORE INFORMATION,
SEE YOUR LOCAL MUSIC DEALER,
OR WRITE TO:

HAL•LEONARD®
CORPORATION
7777 W. BLUEMOUND RD. P.O. BOX 13819
MILWAUKEE, WISCONSIN 53213

Visit Hal Leonard Online at **www.halleonard.com**

0707

NOTE-FOR-NOTE KEYBOARD TRANSCRIPTIONS

These outstanding collections feature note-for-note transcriptions from the artists who made the songs famous. No matter what style you play, these books are perfect for performers or students who want to play just like their keyboard idols.

ACOUSTIC PIANO BALLADS

16 acoustic piano favorites: Angel • Candle in the Wind • Don't Let the Sun Go Down on Me • Endless Love • Imagine • It's Too Late • Let It Be • Mandy • Ribbon in the Sky • Sailing • She's Got a Way • So Far Away • Tapestry • You Never Give Me Your Money • You've Got a Friend • Your Song.
00690351 / $19.95

ELTON JOHN

18 of Elton John's best songs: Bennie and the Jets • Candle in the Wind • Crocodile Rock • Daniel • Don't Let the Sun Go Down on Me • Goodbye Yellow Brick Road • I Guess That's Why They Call It the Blues • Little Jeannie • Rocket Man • Your Song • and more!
00694829 / $20.95

THE BEATLES KEYBOARD BOOK

23 Beatles favorites, including: All You Need Is Love • Back in the U.S.S.R. • Come Together • Get Back • Good Day Sunshine • Hey Jude • Lady Madonna • Let It Be • Lucy in the Sky with Diamonds • Ob-La-Di, Ob-La-Da • Oh! Darling • Penny Lane • Revolution • We Can Work It Out • With a Little Help from My Friends • and more.
00694827 / $20.95

THE CAROLE KING KEYBOARD BOOK

16 of King's greatest songs: Beautiful • Been to Canaan • Home Again • I Feel the Earth Move • It's Too Late • Jazzman • (You Make Me Feel) Like a Natural Woman • Nightingale • Smackwater Jack • So Far Away • Sweet Seasons • Tapestry • Way Over Yonder • Where You Lead • Will You Love Me Tomorrow • You've Got a Friend.
00690554 / $19.95

CLASSIC ROCK

35 all-time rock classics: Beth • Bloody Well Right • Changes • Cold as Ice • Come Sail Away • Don't Do Me like That • Hard to Handle • Heaven • Killer Queen • King of Pain • Layla • Light My Fire • Oye Como Va • Piano Man • Takin' Care of Business • Werewolves of London • and more.
00310940 / $24.95

POP/ROCK

35 songs, including: Africa • Against All Odds • Axel F • Centerfold • Chariots of Fire • Cherish • Don't Let the Sun Go Down on Me • Drops of Jupiter (Tell Me) • Faithfully • It's Too Late • Just the Way You Are • Let It Be • Mandy • Sailing • Sweet Dreams Are Made of This • Walking in Memphis • and more.
00310939 / $24.95

JAZZ

24 favorites from Bill Evans, Thelonious Monk, Oscar Peterson, Bud Powell, Art Tatum and more. Includes: Ain't Misbehavin' • April in Paris • Autumn in New York • Body and Soul • Freddie Freeloader • Giant Steps • My Funny Valentine • Satin Doll • Song for My Father • Stella by Starlight • and more.
00310941 / $22.95

R&B

35 R&B classics: Baby Love • Boogie on Reggae Woman • Easy • Endless Love • Fallin' • Green Onions • Higher Ground • I'll Be There • Just Once • Money (That's What I Want) • On the Wings of Love • Ribbon in the Sky • This Masquerade • Three Times a Lady • and more.
00310942 / $24.95

THE BILLY JOEL KEYBOARD BOOK

16 mega-hits from the Piano Man himself: Allentown • And So It Goes • Honesty • Just the Way You Are • Movin' Out • My Life • New York State of Mind • Piano Man • Pressure • She's Got a Way • Tell Her About It • and more.
00694828 / $22.95

STEVIE WONDER

14 of Stevie's most popular songs: Boogie on Reggae Woman • Hey Love • Higher Ground • I Wish • Isn't She Lovely • Lately • Living for the City • Overjoyed • Ribbon in the Sky • Send One Your Love • Superstition • That Girl • You Are the Sunshine of My Life • You Haven't Done Nothin'.
00306698 / $21.95

Prices, contents and availability subject to change without notice.

FOR MORE INFORMATION, SEE YOUR LOCAL MUSIC DEALER, OR WRITE TO:

HAL•LEONARD® CORPORATION
7777 W. BLUEMOUND RD. P.O. BOX 13819 MILWAUKEE, WI 53213

Visit Hal Leonard online at www.halleonard.com

0107

KEYBOARD *signature licks*

These exceptional book/CD packs teach keyboardists the techniques and styles used by popular artists from yesterday and today. Each folio breaks down the trademark riffs and licks used by these great performers.

BEST OF BEBOP PIANO

by Gene Rizzo

16 bebop piano transcriptions: April in Paris • Between the Devil and the Deep Blue Sea • I Don't Stand a Ghost of a Chance • If I Were a Bell • Lullaby of Birdland • On a Clear Day (You Can See Forever) • Satin Doll • Thou Swell • and more.
00695734..$19.95

CONTEMPORARY CHRISTIAN

by Todd Lowry

Learn the trademark keyboard styles and techniques of today's top contemporary Christian artists. 12 songs, including: Fool for You (Nichole Nordeman) • The Great Divide (Point of Grace) • His Strength Is Perfect (Steven Curtis Chapman) • How Beautiful (Twila Paris) • If I Stand (Rich Mullins) • Know You in the Now (Michael Card) • and more.
00695753..$19.95

BILL EVANS

by Brent Edstrom

12 songs from pianist Bill Evans, including: Five • One for Helen • The Opener • Peace Piece • Peri's Scope • Quiet Now • Re: Person I Knew • Time Remembered • Turn Out the Stars • Very Early • Waltz for Debby • 34 Skidoo.
00695714..$22.95

BEN FOLDS FIVE

by Todd Lowry

16 songs from four Ben Folds Five albums: Alice Childress • Battle of Who Could Care Less • Boxing • Brick • Don't Change Your Plans • Evaporated • Kate • The Last Polka • Lullabye • Magic • Narcolepsy • Philosophy • Song for the Dumped • Underground.
00695578..$22.95

BILLY JOEL CLASSICS: 1974-1980

by Robbie Gennet

15 popular hits from the '70s by Billy Joel: Big Shot • Captain Jack • Don't Ask Me Why • The Entertainer • Honesty • Just the Way You Are • Movin' Out (Anthony's Song) • My Life • New York State of Mind • Piano Man • Root Beer Rag • Say Goodbye to Hollywood • Scenes from an Italian Restaurant • She's Always a Woman • The Stranger.
00695581..$22.95

BILLY JOEL HITS: 1981-1993

by Todd Lowry

15 more hits from Billy Joel in the '80s and '90s: All About Soul • Allentown • And So It Goes • Baby Grand • I Go to Extremes • Leningrad • Lullabye (Goodnight, My Angel) • Modern Woman • Pressure • The River of Dreams • She's Got a Way • Tell Her About It • This Is the Time • Uptown Girl • You're Only Human (Second Wind).
00695582..$22.95

ELTON JOHN CLASSIC HITS

by Todd Lowry

10 of Elton's best are presented in this book/CD pack: Blue Eyes • Chloe • Don't Go Breaking My Heart • Don't Let the Sun Go Down on Me • Ego • I Guess That's Why They Call It the Blues • Little Jeannie • Sad Songs (Say So Much) • Someone Saved My Life Tonight • Sorry Seems to Be the Hardest Word.
00695688..$22.95

LENNON & McCARTNEY HITS

by Todd Lowry

Features 15 hits from A-L for keyboard by the legendary songwriting team of John Lennon and Paul McCartney. Songs include: All You Need Is Love • Back in the U.S.S.R. • The Ballad of John and Yoko • Because • Birthday • Come Together • A Day in the Life • Don't Let Me Down • Drive My Car • Get Back • Good Day Sunshine • Hello, Goodbye • Hey Jude • In My Life • Lady Madonna.
00695650..$22.95

LENNON & McCARTNEY FAVORITES

by Todd Lowry

16 more hits (L-Z) from The Beatles: Let It Be • The Long and Winding Road • Lucy in the Sky with Diamonds • Martha My Dear • Ob-La-Di, Ob-La-Da • Oh! Darling • Penny Lane • Revolution 9 • Rocky Raccoon • She's a Woman • Strawberry Fields Forever • We Can Work It Out • With a Little Help from My Friends • The Word • You're Going to Lose That Girl • Your Mother Should Know.
00695651..$22.95

BEST OF ROCK

by Todd Lowry

12 songs are analyzed: Bloody Well Right (Supertramp) • Cold as Ice (Foreigner) • Don't Do Me Like That (Tom Petty & The Heartbreakers) • Don't Let the Sun Go Down on Me (Elton John) • I'd Do Anything for Love (Meat Loaf) • Killer Queen (Queen) • Lady Madonna (The Beatles) • Light My Fire (The Doors) • Piano Man (Billy Joel) • Point of No Return (Kansas) • Separate Ways (Journey) • Werewolves of London (Warren Zevon).
00695751..$19.95

BEST OF ROCK 'N' ROLL PIANO

by David Bennett Cohen

12 of the best hits for piano are presented in this pack. Songs include: At the Hop • Blueberry Hill • Brown-Eyed Handsome Man • Charlie Brown • Great Balls of Fire • Jailhouse Rock • Lucille • Rock and Roll Is Here to Stay • Runaway • Tutti Frutti • Yakety Yak • You Never Can Tell.
00695627..$19.95

BEST OF STEVIE WONDER

by Todd Lowry

This book/CD pack includes musical examples, lessons, biographical notes, and more for 14 of Stevie Wonder's best songs. Features: I Just Called to Say I Love You • My Cherie Amour • Part Time Lover • Sir Duke • Superstition • You Are the Sunshine of My Life • and more.
00695605..$22.95

Prices, contents and availability subject to change without notice.

0304